❖ **Why They Became Famous** ❖

NAPOLEON BONAPARTE

❖ **Why They Became Famous** ❖

NAPOLEON BONAPARTE

Donnali Shor

Illustrated by Severino Baraldi

Silver Burdett Company

ACKNOWLEDGMENTS

We would like to thank Professor J.K. Sowards, Department of History, Wichita State University for his guidance and helpful suggestions.

Library of Congress Cataloging-in-Publication Data

Shor, Donnali.
  Napoleon Bonaparte.

  (Why they became famous)
  Bibliography: p.
  Includes index.
  Summary: Examines the life of the military genius who crowned himself Emperor of the French and established a vast European empire.
  1. Napoleon, I, Emperor of the French, 1769-1821—Juvenile literature. 2. France—Kings and rulers—Biography—Juvenile literature. |1. Napoleon, I, Emperor of the French, 1769–1821. 2. Kings, queens, rulers, etc.| I. Baraldi, Severino, ill. II. Title. III. Series.

  DC203.S54 1987   944.05'092'4 |B| |92| 86-42627
  ISBN 0-382-09165-5 (lib. bdg.)
  ISBN 0-382-09170-1 (pbk.)

Imprime: Edime, Organización Gráfica, S. A. - Móstoles (Madrid)
Depósito legal: M. 34.742-1986
Impreso en España - Printed in Spain

© Gruppo Editoriale Fabbri, S.p.A 1987

English text written by Donnali Shor

First published in the United States by Silver Burdett Company under license of Gruppo Editoriale Fabbri S.p.A.

CONTENTS

At the Royal Military School

Corsica is a rugged island in the Mediterranean, which lies sixty miles off the coast of Italy. The Corsicans are proud and independent people. In 1768, when the French took over the island from Genoa, an Italian state, the Corsicans rebelled and fought for their freedom. But they were unsuccessful. Their leader, Pasquale Paoli, was driven into exile.

Several months later, on August 15, 1769, Napoleon Bonaparte was born in Ajaccio, a major port on the island. His real name was Napoleone Buonaparte, but as a young man, he decided to give his name a French spelling. He did this because he had his mind set on a military career in France, and he didn't want his Italian-sounding name to stop his progress. In 1796, he changed it permanently to Napoleon Bonaparte.

His parents, Carlo and Letizia, were a handsome young couple. Carlo was eighteen and his bride only fourteen when they married. Their firstborn son was called Joseph. They christened their second born Napoleon because it was a tradition in their family to give second-born sons that name.

Though the Bonapartes came from an aristocratic Italian family, they were poor. They had six more children, which made life even harder for the young couple. Moreover, what little money they could scrape together was often quickly spent by Carlo. He had a great deal of charm but he was weak. His strong-willed wife was the mainstay of the family. Letizia was loving but stern. None of her eight children dared to cross her.

During the day Napoleon and his brother Joseph liked to wander in the hills near their home. In Corsica the hills sometimes lead right down to the beach. The two boys loved to race down the slopes and then, at the bottom of a hill, stop sharply so they wouldn't tumble into the surf. They knew their mother would be angry if they came home with their clothes wet and sandy. Joseph was the more cautious of the two. Napoleon would tear down the hills at break-neck speed, and each time he risked falling into the water. He liked the thrill of hearing the wind whiz past his ears and of feeling his heart beat faster and faster as he flew down to the beach.

The boys' favorite hill was also the steepest. One day they went to the top and started racing down to the surf. As usual, Napoleon was far out ahead. Though he was younger and small for his age, he was very strong and aggressive. He kept on running until he nearly soaked his shoes in the pounding waves.

"I won! I won!" he shouted.

Triumphantly, he turned back to wave to his brother. Then he saw Joseph being beaten up by three bullies. One had a stick. Another was lunging at Joseph, and a third was hitting him with his fists. Joseph's shirt was torn. Furious, Napoleon ran up the hill.

"Why are you hitting my brother?" he asked angrily.

"What are you going to do about it?" mocked one of the boys.

He was the biggest of the three, but Napoleon didn't hesitate. Napoleon pounced on him and with a hard blow to the head, knocked him down. Once the boy was on the ground, Napoleon beat him ferociously. Terrified, the other two boys ran away.

"Don't ever hit my brother again or I'll kill you!" Napoleon shouted, as he kept punching until the boy finally lay motionlessly on the ground.

Later, when his mother heard about what had happened, she didn't seem surprised. "Napoleon's a born fighter," she said proudly.

Despite their poverty, Letizia saw that her children had a happy and carefree childhood. Napoleon went to the parish school and learned to read. Though he became a voracious reader and studied a great deal on his own, in school he was only an average student.

When Napoleon was nine and Joseph ten, their father decided they should go to school in France to get an education befitting their birth. But he didn't have the money to pay for their schooling. He petitioned the king, Louis XVI, for a scholarship for Napoleon. The king had set up a special fund for the sons of French nobles, granting them money to attend military school. Now that Corsica belonged to France, the Bonapartes were French citizens and were eligible for this scholarship.

Napoleon was called into his father's study. The boy was eager to learn why his father wanted to see him. It was rare for his father even to be home; he was usually out socializing with friends.

"Napoleon," said his father seriously, "you have a great opportunity to bring honor to our family. I am sending you to the Royal Military School at Brienne in northern France. You will have the chance to train as a soldier and make us all proud of you!"

Napoleon's eyes lit up. He began to jump up and down with joy. "I will, Papa," he declared. "I want to be a soldier!"

His father smiled, saying, "I know you do, and I am sure you will be a fine soldier someday. You will have many years of studying at Brienne. It is a training school for the Military College in Paris. At Brienne you will get the basic education you will need to be well prepared for the college. Your fellow students will be competing with you for a place there too, but remember that only the best ones will be selected."

"I'll work hard!" promised Napoleon.

Joseph was also going to France with Napoleon. He was planning to enter a Catholic seminary. Both boys were excited about their future. Still, they were apprehensive. They had never left the island before, and they didn't know how to speak French. At home the Bonapartes only spoke Corsican, which was a dialect of Italian, and French was not taught in the boys' local school. Before they could further their training, they would have to learn the language. To do this, their parents were sending them first to a school in Autun in southern France.

Their few possessions were bundled up. Both boys tried to act brave when they set sail for France. They laughed and waved as the sailors rowed them out to the ship that was to take them away from Corsica. They shouted happy good-byes to their mother and to their brothers and sisters. Yet they were sad as they watched their beloved island recede in the distance.

Napoleon didn't return to Corsica or see his family again for eight years. Napoleon and his brother separated after three months at Autun. Joseph wept, but Napoleon, though he felt just as miserable, shed only one tear. He was becoming resigned to the hardships of his new life. While he was at Autun, Napoleon had longed for the sun and sea of his home. In France, it never seemed to stop raining. For days at a time, he had been confined to his small, damp room at the school. Worse, the other students had laughed at his Corsican accent and mocked his poor clothes and rough manners.

When he arrived at Brienne, he found that the students there were even crueler. The sons of French aristocrats, they looked down on him because he was of Corsican nobility. Taunting Napoleon, they called him a "slave" because his home had been conquered by the French.

Napoleon was very sensitive. He withdrew more and more into himself. Soon he stopped trying to make friends. In a corner of the schoolyard, he set up a private garden, which he closed off with a wooden fence. On one of its stakes he nailed a sign that read "Napoleon's Country."

He spent his days there, reading one book after another. The other students knew better than to come near his garden. Anyone who dared to was immediately warned with a scowl to leave. One student, though, decided to challenge Napoleon. While his companions egged him on, he barged into the garden and started to tear it apart.

"Na-po-le-on, Na-po-le-on," jeered the other students.

Napoleon, who had been reading, sprang to his feet.

"Stop!" he shouted. "Get out of my country or you'll regret it!"

The boy laughed. "The Corsican Count is going to beat me up!" he called out to his friends.

With a vicious look in his eye, Napoleon threw himself at the boy. He sent him hurtling through the fence, splintering it in several places. The boy sprawled on the ground. Jumping on him, Napoleon pummeled him with his fists until the boy gave up; then Napoleon let him go.

The boy limped back to his friends. They made fun of him for letting Napoleon beat him up, but from that point on, Napoleon was never again disturbed in his garden.

His teachers also noticed Napoleon's determined and violent character. One wrote about him, "The youngster is made of granite, but there is a volcano inside."

Napoleon intimidated students and teachers alike. He was strong-willed and ambitious. As the years at Brienne went by, he slowly gained the respect of his fellow students. Yet he remained a loner and didn't try to make friends.

Napoleon's favorite books were histories of the great conquerors. He spent hours memorizing the battle dates and conquests of Julius Caesar and Alexander the Great. He read about Hannibal's trek over the Alps with his army and also about the French emperor Charlemagne's rule over Europe. These were his heroes. All his life he liked to read history books, especially those that dealt with military history.

Napoleon dreamed of freeing his home from the French. His ambition was to rule Corsica. Imagining himself as its liberator, he vowed to drive out the French, succeeding where the Corsican patriot Paoli had failed.

Though Napoleon acquired a deep knowledge of many subjects by studying on his own, he was not a brilliant student. Only in mathematics did he distinguish himself. He was also good in history and geography, and showed a talent for military science. But he struggled through his Latin and French courses, and he consistently received lower grades because his handwriting and spelling were terrible.

The winter of 1783 proved especially severe in France. Heavy snows blanketed the fields around Brienne. Throughout the winter the students arranged huge snowball fights. The entire academy of 150 pupils split into two groups. Napoleon was always elected the head of one of the groups because his tactics usually brought victory. Often the students would fight among themselves to be on his team.

Before one snowball fight, he brought together his squad of seventy-five boys. He'd been learning about fortifications in his military science class and was eager to put the material from his lessons into practical use.

"First," he said, "I'm going to split you into two divisions. There will be an attack team and a defense team. I'll lead the attack squad against the enemy. While we're busy with the attack I want the defense team to prepare a huge supply of snowballs. Keep on making them until I tell you to stop. Then I'll give you new orders."

"Why not now?" grumbled one student.

"Because now I want you to make snowballs," shot back Napoleon.

He split the boys into two divisions. With a war yell, he led the attack against the enemy team. Snowballs rained on the yard. Several students were knocked down by the volleys. The boys shouted and laughed. But Napoleon was serious. He aimed his snowballs with deadly force. After ten minutes he whispered to the members of his squad to keep up their attack for another quarter hour. He went back to check on the progress of the defense team. They had worked hard and piled up an enormous mound of snowballs.

"Good work," he said with relish. "All we have to do now is to build the fort and the enemy will be ours."

Napoleon gave exact instructions on how the snow fort should be built, overseeing every detail. When work was progressing to his satisfaction, he rejoined his attack squad. They shouted to him with excitement that they were winning. Napoleon praised them, but to their surprise, he ordered them to retreat. A few boys complained. Even though they trusted his judgment, sometimes they wished he would reveal his game plan.

Nevertheless, they obeyed his order and retreated. The enemy team pursued them. They thought Napoleon's side had lost and was giving up. Yelling with delight, the enemy chased after

Napoleon's squad, pounding them with snowballs. Their entire team attacked in full force against Napoleon's.

"Fire!" Napoleon commanded his squad, when the charging enemy had nearly reached the snow fort.

Fifty snowballs answered his call. The enemy team was caught off guard. Protected by the fort, Napoleon's defense squad kept on bombarding them with snowballs. When his attack squad doubled back, the enemy team realized they had fallen into a well-planned trap, gave up, and fled in all directions.

In 1784, when Napoleon was only fifteen, he graduated from Brienne. He was ranked forty second in a class of fifty-eight students. He was able to pass the required stringent entrance exams for entry into the prestigious Military College in Paris. He was also awarded a scholarship to pay for his expenses at the college.

It was while he was a student at the Military College that he learned of his father's death. Carlo Buonaparte had died of stomach cancer on February 24, 1785. Before his death, the last words he spoke were, "Where is Napoleon, my son Napoleon, whose sword will make kings tremble and who will change the face of the world?"

Revolution

Napoleon's mother was left penniless, with eight children to take care of. Napoleon decided to earn his military commission as quickly as possible so that he could start helping her out financially. Working day and night, he completed the courses at the Military College within the year, though the program usually took two to three years.

At sixteen he graduated with the rank of lieutenant and was assigned to an artillery unit. Napoleon had specialized in artillery at the Military College, because he understood its importance in warfare and wanted to learn how cannons could most effectively be used in battle.

During the next few years he devoted himself to reading about military science, history, and political theory. Napoleon was garrisoned in various cities in France, but he also spent much of his time in Corsica. When he was on military duty, he often worked from four o'clock in the morning until ten at night. Forwarding his meager salary to his mother, he saved only a little to pay for new books for himself. He was so poor he ate only one meal a day.

News from Paris stirred Napoleon as well as the rest of the nation. On July 14, 1789, a mob stormed the Bastille, a prison in the capital. The fortress symbolized the rule of the Bourbons, the royal family. Louis XVI and his Austrian wife, Marie-Antoinette, were resented by the French people because they imposed heavy taxes on them. They were also extravagant and flaunted their power.

Inspired by the American Revolution, the French people rose up against Louis XVI. In various parts of the country, they rioted against high taxation. Eventually, the fall of the Bastille came to symbolize the beginning of the French Revolution.

Despite the unrest, the Royalists were confident they would maintain their power. Supported by the wealthy aristocratic class, they seemed to have the means to crush the rebellion. In addition to their own funds, they received money and aid from other European kings, anxious to suppress the popular revolt against the monarchy. These kings reasoned that if the Revolution were successful in France, democratic ideals might spread to their own countries and threaten their rule.

Though the Royalists had the means, they didn't have the fervor of the mobs, bent on ridding their country of tyranny. The aristocrats were outnumbered because they made up only a small minority of the French population. Ultimately the revolutionary forces defeated the Royalists.

In 1792, France was proclaimed a republic. But the victory for the Republicans came after much bloodshed. Thousands from both sides died in the struggle. Many people were sent to the guillotine during the Revolution. On January 21, 1793, the king himself was executed, and the following October his wife was beheaded.

The end of the monarchy brought forward two revolutionary factions. The first, led by moderates, wanted only gradual reforms. But it was soon overpowered by the radical faction, headed by Maximilien Robespierre. The radicals were known as Jacobins. Though Napoleon didn't agree with their most extreme proposals, he sympathized with their beliefs. He became an active member of the Jacobin movement.

The events of the last years left a deep impression on Napoleon. Moved whenever he saw the tricolor flag of revolutionary France, he took to heart its motto: Liberty, Equality, Fraternity. Napoleon believed in the democratic ideals of the revolutionaries. He believed, for example, that talent rather than birth should determine one's place in society. His wide reading led him to the French philosopher Rousseau, who argued that social injustice should be wiped out. Napoleon became a great admirer of the philosopher.

Throughout his life, Napoleon saw himself as a "child of the Revolution," molded by the ideas of equality and individual freedom fought for during the revolutionary era. Even when he became the absolute ruler of France, he decided that his reign was preserving the ideals of the French Revolution.

When the king was sent to the guillotine in 1793, Napoleon realized a new era had begun for France. However, he didn't consider himself French. His home was Corsica, and he vowed to establish the island as an independent democratic state, under his leadership.

To fulfill his dream, he had returned to Corsica in 1791. His brother Joseph had given up the priesthood to enter Corsican politics. With Joseph's help, Napoleon won a commission as a lieutenant colonel in the Corsican National Guard. Once home, he encouraged his younger brother, Lucien, to join the Jacobins. Together they were active in local politics, agitating for a democratic Corsica that would be governed according to Jacobin principles.

Though Napoleon believed that there was a chance Corsica might be completely independent, he accepted French rule. The brothers thought Corsica could be a self-governing member of the French Empire.

Their beliefs led them to clash with Pasquale Paoli, who had returned to the island after years of exile in England. Paoli also wanted a free Corsica, but he was against the radical reforms proposed by the two brothers, and he opposed all ties with the French Republic.

Paoli was revered by the Corsicans. Soon he swayed them to his point of view. Paoli accused the Bonapartes of being turncoats. Even though Napoleon's father had fought for Corsica's independence from Genoa, Paoli recalled that he had betrayed the Nationalist cause by siding with the French occupiers, once it became clear that the French were going to take over the island. Paoli also charged that Bonaparte's sons had benefited from an education intended for French nobles.

The Corsican patriot further declared that Napoleon's true interest in liberating the island was to be its first ruler. Hearing this, Napoleon's brother Lucien secretly agreed. He found Napoleon's attitude toward democracy contradictory, because Napoleon was contemptuous of the people fighting for it, even though he was a fervent supporter of the Revolution.

Lucien recalled his brother's description of King Louis XVI. On a trip back to France, Napoleon had seen a mob storming the Palace of the Tuileries on June 20, 1792.

"The king appeared on the balcony of the palace," Napoleon recounted. With disgust, he said, "He was wearing the red cap of the revolutionaries on his head. What a ridiculous sight! He thought the mob wouldn't kill him if he showed he was sympathetic to their cause. But he could have killed the whole lot of them if he'd lined up cannons at the palace and opened fire." Scornfully, Napoleon added, "If he had, he would still be king today!"

Lucien thought his brother was too domineering. Even at home, he was in the habit of ordering all his brothers and sisters around. Lucien wrote about him, "We never argued with him. The slightest criticism annoyed him, and the faintest opposition threw him into a rage. I have always detected in Napoleon an ambition that overcomes his desire for the public good. I believe that in a free society he would be a dangerous man. He seems to have the attributes of a tyrant, and I believe he would be one if he were king."

Napoleon's hopes to be Corsica's first ruler were dashed in 1793. Stirred up by the Bonapartes' campaign against Paoli, the Jacobin government in Paris put out an order for Paoli's arrest. Outraged, the Corsicans revolted. Paoli declared the island independent and ordered the immediate arrest of all pro-French Corsicans, singling out the Bonapartes.

Brandishing torches, a mob of Corsicans rushed to attack them. Calling them traitors, the Corsicans smashed the windows of their home with the butt ends of torches. Once the windows were opened, the Corsicans climbed over the sills and rampaged through the Bonapartes' house. But the family had already escaped from the island by boat. From the deck they tearfully watched as the mob set fire to their home. As they sailed away, for several miles they could still see the smoke rise up in angry billows from the island.

First Victory

Napoleon fled Corsica on June 11, 1793. If the Corsicans didn't want his leadership, he declared, he would make France his permanent home. He settled his family near the southern city of Marseilles and then returned to his artillery unit in the north. By this time, Napoleon was a captain, but his salary was still very low. Whatever money he saved, he sent to his mother.

However, he didn't plan on having many more years of hardship. He burned with ambition and plotted ways he could rise in the French military. His break came by way of a lucky accident. He was in Marseilles on military duty when a revolt against the Jacobin government broke out in the Mediterranean port city of Toulon. Napoleon was called into action to replace an artillery officer who had been wounded in battle. He was appointed commander of the artillery forces. His superior, General Carteaux, briefed Napoleon on the siege of Toulon.

"For the past few years," he said, "the Royalists have been rebelling here. Southern France has been their stronghold throughout the Revolution. The British and the Spanish are giving them help because they want to restore the monarchy."

"Or to conquer our country," interrupted Napoleon brusquely.

The general's eyebrows shot up. He was disturbed by Napoleon's domineering manner, but he went on, "In any case, the British seized Toulon in August and captured our fleet. Their ships have been strangling our harbor for the last several months." Pointing to a map, he continued, "This is the fort of L'Eguillette, at the tip of the cape."

"Who controls it?" asked Napoleon eagerly.

"The British," replied General Carteaux with surprise.

"We can destroy them if we take the fort. Let me have all the cannons available and I'll capture Toulon in less than a week!"

At first the general didn't listen to Napoleon. The general was reluctant to put his tactics into action. General Carteaux wasn't as sure of victory as Napoleon was. And while he hesitated, Napoleon assumed power. Ruthlessly, he commandeered all the cannons and soldiers he needed for the attack. Napoleon ordered his men to bombard the fort of L'Eguillette. Soon it was his. Now that he controlled the key position in the harbor, he told his men to aim for the British ships. Realizing he could destroy their fleet, the British abandoned Toulon.

The city fell on December 19, 1793. Napoleon had captured it in less than three days. Next he decided to crush the French Royalists by pursuing all those who opposed the Jacobin government.

He rallied his troops, shouting, "Soldiers! Are we going to let our Republic fall?"

"No! Long live the Republic!"

"The cities of Bordeaux, Marseilles, and Lyons have expelled our forces. Will the spirit of democracy also be expelled from France?"

"No!" thundered the troops.

"Will we allow the Royalists to destroy us? Will we surrender all our victories?"

"Down with traitors! Down with tyranny!" they cried.

Satisfied that he'd stirred his men to a feverish pitch, Napoleon urged them to hunt down all the Royalists of Toulon. He had learned how to manipulate his soldiers, and he took pleasure in commanding them. He enjoyed exercising power. But although he was single-minded in his own drive for authority, he still believed in the democratic ideals of the Revolution.

His soldiers were devoted to him. Napoleon inspired them with his desire for victory. His great self-confidence spurred them on. They also liked his willingness to share the hardships of their lives. During the battle of Toulon, he had been constantly at their side. He'd barely slept. Whenever he became too tired, he rolled himself up in his overcoat and lay on the ground for a quick nap, never sleeping more than a few minutes at a time.

The soldiers also appreciated his concern for them. Daily, he inspected his troops and suggested improvements for his men. Napoleon had a gift for organization. He solved all problems, however great, swiftly and efficiently. Very attentive to details, he made sure his orders were carried out exactly.

Napoleon believed that neglecting small details could make a difference in the outcome of a battle. He wrote, "Only with care and foresight can we achieve great ends. It's but a step from victory to defeat. In important matters I have learned that, finally, everything turns on a trifle."

In addition to decisiveness, Napoleon had another trait that made him popular with his soldiers — he had an amazing memory. Napoleon never forgot anything he ever learned. Once he knew a man's name and background, he remembered the information. He could address thousands of his soldiers by name. They appreciated his personal interest in them whenever he asked about their homes and families.

Napoleon inspired revolutionary fervor in his soldiers at Toulon because he wanted the Royalists driven out of France. He fiercely believed in the Republic and thought the Royalist uprisings were dangerous to its welfare. Still, Napoleon was horrified by the massacre that took place after the siege of Toulon. The Jacobins rounded up all the city's Royalists in the public square, and then executed them, shooting them down with cannons filled with grapeshot.

Napoleon did not approve of these tactics against the rebels, but he was afraid the Royalist uprisings would threaten the new Jacobin republic if they weren't stopped. Provence, a region in the south of France, had already declared itself independent and had established its own government. If the Royalist victories, supported by the British, continued, the country could again become a monarchy. Worse yet, if the political instability in France increased, he thought the nation would grow weak and be ripe for invasion.

Napoleon's capture of Toulon brought him to the attention of the Jacobin leaders in Paris. They praised his quick action against the British. In gratitude they promoted him to the rank of brigadier general.

Napoleon was only twenty-four. He was one of the youngest generals in France. Victorious, he envisioned a great career in the French military.

However, his new rank brought jealousy in its wake. His fellow officers begrudged him his promotion, and some of his superiors hinted that he was more interested in his personal advancement than in the good of the Republic. He was too ambitious, they said.

Nevertheless, he found favor with the Jacobin ministers in Paris. One of them, Augustin Robespierre, wrote to his brother, Maximilien, about Napoleon's brilliant capture of Toulon.

This recommendation nearly cost Napoleon his life. Though Maximilien Robespierre had been one of the most prominent leaders of the Revolution, he was now hated throughout France, because under his leadership, forty thousand people had been sent to the guillotine.

The Royalists still threatened the Republic he had fought so hard to establish; they wanted France to be ruled by a king again. Fearful that they would take over the country, Robespierre ordered the execution of all those who opposed his rule. Some people were sent to the guillotine without benefit of trial. Anyone who was accused of being against the Republic risked immediate death. Because of this policy, a number of innocent men and women had also been executed.

This period in French history became known as the Reign of Terror. To preserve the Republic, the Jacobins took desperate measures to crush their opposition. Their harsh laws resulted in riots throughout France. Also, food shortages caused by the domestic turmoil led to starvation in some parts of the country.

Deciding to overthrow Robespierre and his radical followers, the moderates seized power on July 27, 1794. Both Maximilien and his brother, Augustin, were arrested and condemned to death by guillotine.

Their death ended the Reign of Terror. A period of political upheaval followed. The moderates, anxious to restore stability in France, ordered the execution of all radical Jacobins active in France.

Some of Napoleon's fellow officers denounced him to the authorities. Jealous of his promotion to brigadier general, they accused him of being a personal favorite of Maximilien Robespierre. Arrested on his return from a military mission to Genoa, he was put in prison in Fort Carré at Antibes on August 8, 1794.

Napoleon's cell was damp and smelled of mildew. The light from his candle made the beads of moisture dripping from the walls glisten. At night he could hear mice run across the floors of the prison. Even though it was already mid-August, it was chilly in his cell.

Napoleon was furious. Each day he loudly demanded his release. Was this how France rewarded her generals, he roared?

He decided to appeal to the government for his freedom. While he was writing, he saw the face of his Corsican friend Jean-Christophe Saliceti appear through the bars of his cell. With a cry of joy, Napoleon rose to meet him. They had been together at Toulon and were very close.

"Be quiet," whispered Saliceti. Looking around anxiously, he said, "No one knows I'm here. I've been trying to get you out of prison for the past week. If you're not released soon, you'll be sent to the guillotine. The new government isn't showing any mercy. All of Robespierre's followers are being executed. And it's all being done fast to destroy the Jacobins as quickly as possible."

"It won't make any difference that I wasn't a radical," said Napoleon bitterly. "I'll never have a trial to prove my innocence, so there's no point in worrying about justice. I'll just be sent to the guillotine." Then, with a defiant shake of his head, he declared, "The only solution is a direct appeal to the government. Go to Paris, Saliceti. Convince them there's no evidence against me. Be sure to say that France needs me. Since most of the military officers were executed during the Revolution because they were Royalists, tell the government they need trained men like me now more than ever to build a strong Republican army. While you do that, I'll write them a petition asking for my release."

To Destiny

Their joint appeal to the government was successful. On August 20, 1794, Napoleon received word that he had been cleared of all charges. He was immediately set free.

However, Napoleon's career suffered a setback. On his release he was transferred to the infantry, and assigned a job in the map-drawing department, which humiliated him. He complained that he was a man of action and had proved his leadership on the battlefield. But his military superiors stopped all his attempts to win a military commission, because they resented him and did not want him to rise in the ranks.

Napoleon decided to ask the government directly for an active command.

"Corsica has fallen to the Paolists," he said. "Now it could fall into the hands of the British. The British have supported Paoli and have an army garrisoned on the island. If we don't drive them out, they may take over Corsica. Do you want our enemy to be so close to our border? I urge you to give me an army so that I can rout the British and crush the Paolists. Let me bring Corsica back into our glorious Republic!"

Some government officials balked. They thought his real ambition was to take over the island and set himself up as its king. Nevertheless, Napoleon was appointed the artillery commander of a small fleet to reconquer Corsica. He set sail for the island but was defeated by the British Royal Navy before he ever reached Corsica. All of Napoleon's training had been in land combat. He never proved to be a good naval commander. Throughout his life, his military genius was evident on the battlefield but never at sea.

Defeated, he returned to Paris. He resolved to win a military commission despite his superiors' opposition. Spending his days going from one minister to another, he grew depressed as the months passed, and they refused to give him an active command. Napoleon was even further demoted when his name was put on the reserve list of the military. This meant he was paid only when he was called up for duty. For weeks afterwards, he wandered miserably around the streets of Paris. His face grew haggard and he looked unkempt. Napoleon didn't have enough money to keep his clothes in good condition. His uniform became shabby, and his boots riddled with holes he couldn't repair. Eventually, he even stopped trying to get an active command. He was considering giving up his military career in France altogether when he received an offer to go to Constantinople (now called Istanbul) to join the Sultan's army. Before he could leave for Turkey, however, events in France changed his plans.

France was governed by a body of elected delegates known as the National Convention. The delegates were drawing up a constitution for the new Republic. They were also implementing reforms to change the social structure of France, because under the monarchy, the nobles had many class privileges. The delegates wanted to abolish these special privileges in order to make France a democracy with equal rights for all. But the reforms were slow in coming, and there was much dissatisfaction in France, even among supporters of the Revolution.

To return the country to order, the moderates decided to establish a new form of government which they hoped would be more efficient. It was known as the Directory. Five leaders, called directors, would be in charge of the nation's affairs. In addition there would be two bodies of representatives, the Council of Ancients and the Council of Five Hundred.

But before the directors could be installed, the Convention faced a crisis. The Royalists had continued to agitate against the government in various parts of France. On October 2, 1795, riots broke out in Paris. Angry mobs ran through the streets, protesting against the Convention. The Royalist sympathizers planned to storm the Palace of the Tuileries and overthrow the government. Twenty-five thousand insurgents from Paris and from all parts of the country gathered in the city to march on the palace.

Aware that the mob threatened to topple the government, the Convention met in an emergency session on the night of October 2. At four-thirty the next morning, they appointed Paul-François Barras director of defense. Barras, an aristocrat from southern France, had quickly risen to power during the chaotic years that followed the Revolution. As director of defense he was put in charge of quelling the riots and of reestablishing peace in the city. Barras had little military experience. To effectively destroy the Royalist opposition, he knew he had to rely on a military expert. From his spies he learned that the march on the Tuileries was planned for October 5. He only had a few days to prepare the defense of the government.

Two years before, Barras had been appointed to make an official report on the battle of Toulon. Now, suddenly remembering Napoleon, he decided that Napoleon was the perfect man for the emergency.

"Ask General Bonaparte to come here at once," he ordered. A messenger rushed to get Napoleon for an immediate interview at the Palace of Chaillot. Barras waited impatiently. He'd been impressed by Napoleon's decisive victory over the British at Toulon. His quick capture of the harbor had proved to him that Napoleon was an able strategist. And Barras was convinced that Napoleon could be ruthless with his own countrymen if they opposed the Republic.

When Napoleon was announced, Barras greeted him hurriedly.

"Citizen Bonaparte," he said, "I'm appointing you military commander in defense of the city. Do you accept?"

"Will I have complete command of the army?"

"Yes," answered Barras.

"Then I accept," said Napoleon.

"The insurgents are going to storm the Tuileries in less than two days. If they take the palace, the Republic will be lost."

"How many soldiers are available?" asked Napoleon.

"Five thousand, against twenty-five thousand insurgents."

"That doesn't matter," replied Napoleon firmly. He immediately planned his strategy. Napoleon ordered the cavalry to seize fifty cannons at a garrison five miles from Paris, because he didn't want this artillery to fall into Royalist hands. When the cannons were brought to him, he mounted the defense of the Tuileries.

"Soldiers! I want half the cannons placed in all the avenues leading up to the Tuileries and on top of all the tallest buildings near the palace. The rest I want mounted on the bridges of the Seine and in the square in front of the Tuileries."

First he supervised the placement of the cannons, and then he assigned his soldiers to their posts. He made sure that all the approaches to the Tuileries had been secured. When everything was ready, he waited.

On October 5 the Royalists began swarming down the avenues leading up to the palace. Armed with clubs and muskets, they shouted "Long live the king!" as they advanced. Napoleon ordered his men to fire. The cannons made a loud roar. Grapeshot scattered over the mob, mowing down hundreds of people. The rest fled in panic. Less than two hours later, all was quiet.

Napoleon was famous overnight. His bold action, which became known as the "whiff of grapeshot," saved the Republic. On October 16, 1795, the grateful Directory named him a major general. Shortly afterward, he was appointed commander-in-chief of the Army of the Interior. Put in charge of stopping antigovernment riots in France, he was also responsible for defending France from foreign invasions.

Napoleon was only twenty-six years old. He was one of the youngest generals to ever hold such a high position in the history of the country. The Directory gave him full command over all the soldiers garrisoned in France. Since he had the authority to reorganize the army, he set to the task with enthusiasm. Paying attention to the smallest of details, he quickly made the Army of the Interior efficient and ready for combat in case of a foreign invasion.

Napoleon was extremely generous. When he reorganized the army, he awarded his friends and family with high posts in the government. He promoted soldiers who had fought with him at Toulon, giving them high ranks in the army. Napoleon even promoted military officers who had been jealous of him in the past, because he knew he needed to win their support if he wanted to lead an army completely united under his command.

Napoleon's victory over the Royalists ensured there would be no more uprisings for some time. After the long years of bloodshed caused by the Revolution, the people of Paris could finally relax. Gratefully they began celebrating this new era of peace. Throughout the fall of 1795, there were hundreds of public balls given in Paris. The city was enjoying its first months of peace since the fall of the Bastille, six years before.

Napoleon was a hero to the citizens of Paris because he'd made the democratic government secure. They hoped France would grow prosperous under the Directors headed by Barras, who had been appointed director in chief for his role in crushing the Royalists.

One night the two men attended a reception given by a prominent woman of the city, Madame Tallien. Among the guests, Napoleon noticed a beautiful woman who was happily laughing with a cluster of friends. She had an open and gracious manner that seemed to captivate everyone around her. Intrigued, Napoleon asked Barras who she was.

"Her name is Josephine de Beauharnais," replied the Director. "Her husband was a count, but he was executed during the Revolution, when we purged the aristocrats who supported the king. She barely escaped the guillotine herself." Noting Napoleon's eager interest, he added, "She's a Creole from Martinique. Her father was a planter on the island, and she came to Paris at sixteen to marry de Beauharnais. Would you like to meet her?"

"No, thank you," replied Napoleon hastily. "I was only curious."

Barras smiled. He'd noticed that for all of Napoleon's decisiveness in battle, the general was shy with women. Leading him by the arm, Barras presented Napoleon to Josephine. He fell madly in love with her. After a few months of passionate courtship, they married on March 9, 1796. Inside the wedding ring he gave her were engraved the words "To Destiny."

The Young Conqueror

Their honeymoon lasted only two days. It was cut short because Napoleon received orders to head a military expedition against the Austrians in Italy. At that time Italy wasn't yet a unified country. It was made up of several states, some of which were under Austrian rule. The Directory, fearing that the Austrians were planning to march their army across Italy into southern France, sent Napoleon to stop them.

Napoleon's army numbered thirty-eight thousand men. He knew the Austrians had an army twice that size. He had a further problem: the troops that were meant to go to Italy were in disastrous shape. Called the Army of Italy, they were plagued by theft, desertion, and mismanagement. In addition Napoleon faced personal animosity from the other military officers at the camp. They resented him because he'd been placed over their heads even though he was young and inexperienced in battle. Also, his appearance didn't impress them much because he was short and slight. But Napoleon ignored their disapproval. He was confident he would conquer Italy, and he quickly communicated his own sense of power to them. His commanding presence and his obvious military brilliance soon won them over.

Next he had to win over the soldiers. Working around the clock, he brought great changes to their living conditions. He issued over a hundred new regulations to improve the army. The soldiers' morale rose. They began to admire Napoleon, believing he would lead them to victory against the far superior Austrian army. He thrilled them with promises of great conquests.

Napoleon issued proclamations whose fiery language stirred them. In his memoirs he later claimed that his first bulletin to the Army of Italy was this passionate and rousing speech: "Soldiers! You're naked and badly fed. The government owes you a great deal but can give you nothing. Your patience and your courage are admirable, but they don't win you any glory. No fame shines down on you. I want to lead you into the most fertile plains in the world. Rich provinces and great cities will be yours. There you will find glory, honor, and wealth. Soldiers of the Army of Italy, will you lack courage?"

Sure that they would follow him to victory, Napoleon's soldiers marched into Italy. Convinced he could defy and conquer the great Austrian army, they eagerly went into battle. In fourteen days they won six battles. Each victory made them more and more certain of his promise of conquest.

When the French attacked the town of Lodi, Napoleon proved to his men that he too was willing to face enemy fire. To conquer Lodi, the troops had to cross a bridge leading into the town. The Austrians were bombarding it with heavy cannon fire. Oblivious to the danger, Napoleon rushed up to the head of his troops. Waving his sword, he forced his way across the narrow bridge.

"Soldiers!" he cried. "The honor of France is in your hands. Let us march to victory and destroy the Austrian tyrants!"

Admiring his bravery, the soldiers stormed the bridge. Many died, yet he inspired such a fanatical devotion among his troops that they advanced despite the cannon fire and eventually conquered Lodi.

This victory convinced Napoleon that he had a special destiny. Years later he recalled: "It was only on the evening after Lodi that I realized I was a superior being and conceived the ambition of performing great things that, till then, had filled my thoughts only as a fantastic dream."

After his exploit at Lodi, Napoleon became a legendary figure to his men. Inspired by him, they marched across Italy, conquering city after city, and finally driving the Austrians out of the country. Moreover, France's southern border was now secure. Ever since the Revolution the threat of foreign invasion had been constant. France was ringed on all sides by enemies only too

willing to take advantage of its political instability and to conquer it. France's most powerful enemies were Austria and Great Britain. Their rulers were also the most opposed to the democratic regime in France, and they plotted unceasingly for the Republic's downfall.

With his small demoralized army, Napoleon had humiliated the great army of the Austrian Empire. And when the French learned of his victories, they celebrated throughout the country. Each new conquest stirred the people to a greater and greater patriotic fervor.

On his return to Paris, Napoleon was given a hero's welcome. He was greeted with shouts of ''Long live the Republic! Long live Bonaparte!'' Men and women craned their necks to see the young general, who had defeated the Austrians. They flocked to the city's museums to see the hundreds of art treasures he'd seized as the spoils of war. In his honor they petitioned to have the street in front of his house renamed Victory Street.

Napoleon was lionized in France. His victory over the Austrians gave the French people, who had been weary of the political turmoil since the Revolution, a new sense of national pride.

After routing the Austrians, Napoleon decided to take on France's other great enemy, Great Britain. Britain was seizing French islands in the West Indies. Their ships were also sinking French vessels in open waters to prevent the French from trading with other countries. The French navy was too weak to protect French commercial ships at sea and too disorganized to fight against the British navy, which was the most powerful navy in the world.

In the spring of 1798, Napoleon approached the Directors with a novel idea.

"We can't invade England by sea," he told them, "because they would destroy our entire fleet in a matter of days. But I think we can weaken them economically. Their prize colony is India. If we close off their access to it via Egypt, we can cripple their economy; much of their wealth comes from India. If they can't reach it, they will lose a great deal of their resources and won't have goods to trade. Give me an army and I will conquer Egypt, their gateway to India. We will defeat the British, even if we can't attack them directly!"

Funds were immediately approved for his project. Even though it was supposedly carried out in secret, Napoleon's expedition eventually became the talk of Paris. Crowds cheered him wildly whenever he appeared in public. They were excited by the idea of conquering Egypt. They were also looking forward to the Egyptian treasures that Napoleon had promised to send back to the city's museums. Hundreds of scholars were going with him on the expedition to study Egyptian culture, which made the citizens of Paris even more curious about his mission; Egypt seemed exotic to them.

Napoleon was also thrilled by the prospect of capturing Egypt. Like his boyhood heroes, Alexander the Great and Julius Caesar, he wanted to found an empire extending to the Orient. Egypt was going to be the first step.

"I want to conquer the world!" he declared to a friend. "Little Europe is just a molehill. Great fame can only be won by conquering the East!"

With visions of glory, Napoleon sailed for Egypt on May 19, 1798, with an army of forty thousand men. Less than a month later, he made his first conquest, seizing the Mediterranean island of Malta. His forces then set sail for Alexandria in Egypt, arriving there at dawn on July 2. They marched into the city. By nightfall, Alexandria had surrendered to them. Dazzled by these easy victories, Napoleon's men felt sure they could take all of Egypt. Then its riches would be theirs, just as Napoleon had promised.

Eager for plunder, they marched inland along the Nile. They intended to ransack the pyramids. But as the days stretched on, the treasures of Egypt seemed less and less appealing to the

men. The broiling desert heat made them lose their determination to keep on marching. Aware of their unhappiness, Napoleon rode among his troops, firing them with visions of glory, but as soon as he was gone, they became discouraged again.

Exhausted by the torrid desert heat, the men complained about their long march to the pyramids.

"Where are the treasures General Napoleon told us about?" asked one soldier. "All I see is sand for miles and miles."

"And there's no food or water in this country. Just this horrible desert!" added another one bitterly.

"If it's not hunger or thirst that will kill us," broke in a third, swatting away an insect "it'll be the plague." They knew several men had already died from it.

With low spirits, the soldiers trudged on for days, despite the heat and burning sands of the desert. Then on July 21, through the noonday haze, they saw the pyramids at last.

Pointing to them, Napoleon shouted, "Soldiers! From the tops of those pyramids, four thousand years of history are watching you!" He urged them to defeat the Mamelukes, who were guarding the pyramids.

The Mamelukes were Egypt's military class. Originally foreign-born slaves, they had revolted against the Egyptians in the thirteenth century. Seizing power, they ruled Egypt for centuries, until they were conquered by the Turks. The Mamelukes managed to keep their control over the Egyptians by serving the new Turkish rulers. At the time of Napoleon's invasion, Egypt was still part of the Turkish Empire. Under orders from the Turks, the Mamelukes were supposed to drive Napoleon out of the country. They were a colorful army. Wearing jeweled turbans and wielding yataghans, sabers with double-curved blades, they charged against Napoleon's army. But their cavalry was no match for his artillery. They were massacred by the French.

Napoleon's sense of victory was short-lived, however. He learned that on August 1 Lord Nelson had destroyed his entire fleet at Abukir Bay in the mouth of the Nile. Only two of his four hundred ships had survived the British naval attack. Napoleon was cut off from sailing home to France. After a disastrous attempt at an overland route through Palestine and Syria, he decided to withdraw his troops to Egypt and settle down to rule the country until he would be able to get back to France.

Seizing Power

To improve Egyptian life, Napoleon had roads and hospitals built throughout the country. While he tended to the administration of Egypt, his team of scholars did an exhaustive study of Egyptian culture. Among their discoveries was a curious stone found near the town of Rosetta. It had inscriptions in three languages, including Egyptian hieroglyphics. The Rosetta stone, as it become known, eventually made it possible to decipher the ancient Egyptian language.

In August, 1799, Napoleon received word there was trouble at home. The Directory had grown weak and unstable. Austria had recaptured Italy and was one of several nations threatening to invade France. He also learned that the Royalists were again plotting to restore the monarchy.

Napoleon decided it was the perfect time to assume power. The country's instability would make it easy for him to take it over. He thought he could count on a number of important ministers to help him. His brother Lucien would support him as well, he knew. Lucien had risen to the presidency of the Council of Five Hundred, the lower house of representatives. This meant he would be able to convince the elected delegates in the council to back Napoleon, should Napoleon need their political support.

Leaving his troops behind in Egypt, he sailed to France on one of his two remaining ships. On his arrival he was given a triumphant welcome and hailed as the conqueror of Egypt. This played right into his hands. Because he was so popular, the Directory didn't dare criticize him openly, although they were aware he was planning a takeover. While they fumed, Napoleon carefully plotted the coup d'état with his supporters.

Napoleon had two great advantages over his political opponents: he was a national hero and he had the full command of the army, which gave him military backing should it be necessary to

overthrow the government violently. His supporters guessed he was more driven by ambition than by love of country, but they believed that only Napoleon would be a forceful and strong enough leader to unite France and drive the enemy from its borders.

On the morning of November 9, 1799, Napoleon appeared before the Council of Ancients, the upper house of representatives. He convinced them the nation was in a state of emergency. Presenting himself as the defender of the Republic, he asked that they give him command of the Paris garrison so that he could guarantee order. Vowing loyalty to the constitution, he convinced them by making a passionate speech, promising to defend the Republic. They agreed to his proposal. However, he still needed the permission of the Council of Five Hundred. The next day he appeared before them but met a very different reaction because the opposition had had time to rally against him.

"Outlaw!" cried the delegates. "Down with the dictator!"

Shouting "Tyrant!" a Corsican deputy rushed up to Napoleon. He pulled out a knife and threatened to kill him. Other delegates tried to hit Napoleon, but his soldiers managed to escort him safely away from the furious delegates.

"The Council is immediately dissolved because of the violence against General Bonaparte," declared Lucien from the podium.

Using this as a pretext, the two brothers ordered Napoleon's soldiers to march into the assembly to restore order. Scrambling away before the soldiers' bayonets, the delegates surrendered to Napoleon. He was named First Consul of France. He immediately set to work on reorganizing the country. Napoleon reduced taxes, founded the Bank of France to stabilize the economy, opened schools and universities, established public programs to give jobs to the unemployed, and commissioned jurists to draw up a civil code unifying all of France's laws. Known as the Code Napoleon, it became the foundation of the country's legal system and is still in use today.

Tirelessly, Napoleon worked day and night to bring order to France. Sleeping only a few hours a night, he quickly instituted political reforms granting civil rights to the people. Nevertheless, France was no longer a democracy because he hadn't been elected by its citizens. When he assumed power, France became a dictatorship. Those who had fought hardest to establish the Republic during the Revolution were outraged, but the majority of French citizens welcomed his rule, because they could see that his strong, effective leadership was improving the country.

In the spring of 1800, Napoleon received an urgent message from his military officers in Genoa. The Austrian army was planning to march across Italy and invade France. In panic his officers warned him that their troops were in no shape to fight off the enemy.

To drive the Austrians out of Italy permanently, Napoleon conceived a plan, which has gone down in military history as one of the most daring war maneuvers ever attempted.

Napoleon gave his troops an official review near the Swiss border. This convinced Austria's spies in France that he intended to march his troops south to reinforce the army stationed at Genoa. They immediately sent word to their superiors to strengthen Austrian forces in Italy. However, Napoleon wanted to mislead them because he was planning a surprise attack on the Austrian army.

While he was reviewing his troops at the border, he had three separate divisions of soldiers marching secretly into Switzerland. He ordered them to wait for him when they rejoined at the foot of the Alps.

After reviewing his decoy troops, he hurried to meet his waiting soldiers. They shouted with joy when they saw him. Napoleon called together his military officers to assign them their duties. As usual, he had kept his plans secret.

"We will split into four divisions," he told them. "Each of you will lead a division over the Alps."

The officers gasped. Ignoring them, Napoleon continued, "Have your men secure the cannons with rope before we take them across the mountains." Then he gruffly added, "I don't want any lost from negligence. I'll check on each and every one of them before we set out."

Napoleon's officers were shocked. They knew the mountain paths would be narrow and dangerous. How could he expect his men to survive a trek over the snow and ice of the Alps, they wondered. Still, despite their misgivings, no one dared to challenge him.

Napoleon led his command of forty-thousand men over the most dangerous pass of the four, the Great St. Bernard Pass. Like Hannibal centuries before, he was taking an army over the treacherous Alps. Shivering from the cold, his men stumbled through huge snowdrifts. They slid over the ice and lost their footing on the frozen slopes. Cold winds whipped them. Yet they plowed on, encouraged by Napoleon. He rode among them, urging them forward.

"You are the glory of France!" he told his men. "Don't let the Austrians put us in chains! Save your homes and families from Austrian tyranny!"

Napoleon paid special attention to the soldiers dragging the cannons over the snow. Whenever he saw one of them struggle particularly hard, he got off his horse and walked along beside him to give him courage.

"Soldier Hourcade," he called out to one. "The eyes of France are on you! March on!"

Though his tone was stern, the soldier knew Napoleon was concerned about his welfare. Squaring his soldiers, he pulled even harder at the cannon until it was free from the snow. Afterwards, Napoleon praised him for his bravery.

The troops crossed the Alps in five days. Marching into Italy, Napoleon led them into battle against the Austrians near the town of Marengo on June 14, 1800. Expecting to meet his troops weeks later much farther south, the Austrians were surprised and unprepared for battle. Napoleon attacked their rear army, in charge of supplies. He knew the Austrian artillery would be at the front. Just as he had planned, he'd cut the front from its supplies and the rear from its artillery. Despite this advantage, the battle of Marengo was a long, hard contest between the two forces, but Napoleon was finally victorious. He returned in triumph to France.

The Emperor Napoleon

Napoleon's peace terms with the Austrians were severe. He forced them to surrender Belgium, Holland, Luxembourg, the Rhineland, Switzerland and Italy. In one stroke, Napoleon secured France's borders against foreign invasion, because these buffer states would protect France from its enemies. Napoleon asked them to pay war tribute, which replenished France's treasury and strengthened the country's economy.

By exacting these terms, Napoleon proved he was a master statesman as well as a military genius. His strong, decisive leadership was admired throughout France. There was national rejoicing when he escaped injury after an assassination attempt on December 24, 1800.

On that date Napoleon and Josephine were on their way to hear Christmas music. Suddenly a barrel rolled before their carriage. Reining in the frightened horses, the driver of the coach shouted "Watch out!" to the startled people in the street. He jumped off the carriage and kicked the barrel aside. Thinking it looked dangerous, he decided to get away from it as quickly as possible. Cracking his whip, he made his horses go at a gallop.

Minutes later, Napoleon and Josephine heard a tremendous blast and then people screaming. His police later told him that the assassination attempt had injured sixty pedestrians and killed several others.

The threat on his life disturbed Napoleon. He began to think of ways he could keep his control over France permanently. Because he wasn't a king, he didn't have an automatic right to rule. Napoleon knew that the other rulers of Europe, who were all monarchs, didn't consider him their equal. Like them, he wanted a title that would permit his heirs also to rule over the country. However, he knew the French people wouldn't accept his taking the title of king, because it would remind them of the Bourbon kings they had hated so much. If he took that title, it would surely cause an uproar; so many had fought to get rid of the monarchy during the Revolution.

Napoleon was already recognized as one of the most powerful leaders on the Continent. In the United States, too, he was considered the equal of the other European rulers. Thomas Jefferson sent him envoys to buy territory that France owned in America. The land extended from the Gulf of Mexico west to the Rockies. This transaction, which became known as the Louisiana Purchase, nearly doubled the size of the United States.

After much thought, Napoleon found a solution that would allow him to become the absolute ruler of France. In 1804 he decided to have himself named emperor. His conquests had made the title possible. To avoid any objections, Napoleon said he would be like Charlemagne, the great Frankish king who was crowned emperor by the pope in A.D. 800. Napoleon vowed to make France an even more glorious empire than Charlemagne's. Dazzled by his promises, the people overwhelmingly approved of his taking the title of emperor.

The coronation was held on December 2, 1804, at the great Cathedral of Notre Dame in Paris. Napoleon and Josephine arrived in a carriage adorned with gold and crystal.

The crowds in the church whispered with awe when they saw Josephine enter the cathedral. "How beautiful she is," they murmured as she and Napoleon walked up to the altar. Her dress was made of satin. Napoleon's sisters held her heavy train as she bent before the pope. Unlike Charlemagne, Napoleon did not want the pope to crown him emperor. This he undertook to do himself. The magnificent ceremony lasted several hours. At one point, Napoleon turned to his brother Joseph, who was near him, and exclaimed, "If only our father could see us now!"

When it came time for the actual coronation, Napoleon went up to the altar, took the crown, and turned toward the people in the cathedral. Raising the crown high above his head, he presented it to them and then crowned himself. Afterward, he crowned Josephine. The crowds were stunned. Never before had a monarch consecrated himself. Several people worried that it indicated his desire for absolute power over all things, but the rest were soon cheering loudly, "Long live the emperor! Long live the emperor!"

In his first decrees as emperor, Napoleon gave royal titles to his siblings, making them monarchs over the lands he had conquered. Insecure about not being a true monarch, Napoleon felt he needed to prove he was the strongest ruler in Europe in order to maintain his domination over the Continent. The other nations feared his ambition. They decided to band together in an alliance to stop him from conquering any more lands.

The league included Napoleon's two great enemies, Austria and Great Britain. The latter had declared war on France in 1803, accusing Napoleon of repeated aggressions. Napoleon made plans to invade Britain, but the naval attack was stalled several times over the next two years. Frustrated by the superior British navy, Napoleon concentrated on another goal at the same time: he gathered and trained a huge army to defeat the continental powers.

After the league was formed, Napoleon didn't wait for the allied armies to strike. He took the offensive, conscripting thousands more soldiers into his Grand Army. To finance his wars against the league, he exacted even more tribute from the countries in his empire.

The allies immediately began marching against France. As usual, Napoleon decided to strike first. The allied forces had advanced up to the Belgian frontier but were not yet united in their attack against Napoleon. He decided to cut short their advance and fight each of them separately. Napoleon attacked the Prussians first, defeated them, and drove them back. However, confusion among his commanders during the battle prevented him from routing them decisively. This proved to be a fatal mistake. Two days later, on June 18, 1815, his troops attacked the British army at Waterloo in Belgium. Commanded by the Duke of Wellington, the British troops withstood Napoleon's artillery.

Napoleon was confident he would easily beat Wellington's army, because he thought the Prussians would be unable to give the British support during the battle. But as the day wore on, thousands of soldiers from both countries fell on the battlefield, neither side achieving a clear victory. At twilight, however, the Prussians, who had managed to regroup their forces, came to the rescue of their allies. When Napoleon saw them swarming onto the battlefield, he knew that the battle was lost.

Napoleon's attempt to reclaim the throne became known as The Hundred Days, ending with his great defeat at Waterloo.

Napoleon first met the Austrians in battle. Near Ulm in Germany, he demolished their army in 1805. The enemy he hated even more was Great Britain. He wanted to destroy that country's navy so he could finally invade Britain. Napoleon gave orders to his leading naval commander, Admiral Pierre de Villeneuve, to sink a British squadron in the waters off the Antilles. If the admiral succeeded, the French fleet would be equal in number to the powerful British navy, which would give Napoleon a chance at least if the two fleets were to engage in a naval battle.

Admiral Villeneuve knew the British navy under Lord Nelson was far superior to his fleet, yet he didn't dare challenge Napoleon outright. As Napoleon's power had increased, he'd become more and more sure he was invincible. Also, he'd grown so domineering and quick to anger that his military officers were afraid of losing their commissions by contradicting him.

Tentatively Villeneuve said, "Sire, our ships aren't in good condition at the moment. I'm afraid we may lose many men if we go into battle with Lord Nelson."

"Carry out my orders," snapped Napoleon. "Destroy them, however many men and however many ships it takes."

Admiral Villeneuve's fears were justified. His fleet was no match for Lord Nelson's. When his navy met the British in the Antilles, it was driven back across the seas to Spain. To save face with Napoleon, Admiral Villeneuve tried to run the blockade of ships set up by the British to stop him from getting back to France. On October 21, 1805, Lord Nelson attacked him at Trafalgar, off the coast of southwestern Spain. Under Nelson's command, the British reduced the entire French fleet to rubble.

The smashing defeat at Trafalgar ended any hope Napoleon had of invading Great Britain by sea. The British lost their great naval commander, Lord Nelson, who was killed in the battle, but Napoleon lost his navy. He vowed revenge on the British. If he couldn't destroy them by sea, he would beat them on land, he swore.

To admit defeat, Napoleon thought, would give his enemies the chance to conquer him. Only greater and greater victories would keep him supreme as a world leader. He refused to let his enemies relish his defeat at Trafalgar. Napoleon decided to challenge the league of countries against him. He wanted to destroy each power in turn so that all Great Britain's allies would be crushed.

"My power depends on my glory, and my glory on my victories," he declared to a friend. "My power would crumble if I didn't support it with new glory and new victories. Conquest has made me what I am — conquest alone will keep me in power."

Because he had already decimated Austria's army at Ulm, he wanted to annihilate what was left of their forces before he challenged the other nations of the league. Napoleon ordered his troops to march into Vienna and occupy the capital of the Austrian Empire.

The Austrian emperor, Francis I, appealed to Czar Alexander I, the ruler of Russia, for help. When the Czar's forces arrived in Austria, their combined armies were far greater in number than Napoleon's. Confident they would defeat him, they prepared to meet him in battle near the village of Austerlitz in northern Austria.

Napoleon had already staked out his battle positions. In the evening he rode along the front to see how the enemy was arranging their troops. He could see from their campfires where they were located.

Turning to a military officer riding with him, Napoleon said with a smile, "The enemy will be ours by tomorrow night."

Napoleon didn't explain his strategy to the officer. He had no intention of doing so until the next morning when he planned to give his marshals exact instructions for the battle. The night was cold and brisk. Napoleon buttoned the large gray overcoat he often wore in battle. Sure of victory the next day, he calmly looked out over the plains surrounding Austerlitz. The bleak winter landscape was dotted with the light from the flames of enemy campfires. A happy look came over his face as he watched their lights flicker in the distance.

"This is the most wonderful night of my life!" he exclaimed.

At seven o'clock the next morning, he called together his marshals. Napoleon was superstitious. He considered it a good omen that it was a crisp and sunny morning. Cheerfully he bantered with his marshals as they gathered for the meeting. However, they responded stiffly. They were on edge because Napoleon often flew into a rage unexpectedly.

"I've deployed several units of our troops on high ground," he told them. "They'll open fire when we force the enemy to go by them later today." With a satisfied smile, he said, "We'll cut the Russians off from the Austrians, drive the Russians through the pass, and then blast them until they surrender."

His marshals were amazed by his absolute conviction he would win. However, just as he'd predicted, the enemy was forced to surrender by nightfall. It was the greatest victory of his career. The battle of Austerlitz took place on December 2, 1805, which Napoleon thought was a fitting way to observe the anniversary of his first year as emperor.

Defeat in Russia

The battle of Austerlitz destroyed the enemy forces in Austria. The toll of their loss was enormous: eight thousand of their soldiers died and fifteen thousand more were wounded. Napoleon took nearly twenty-three thousand prisoners. What had remained of the weak Austrian army was shattered.

Over the next few years Napoleon waged a string of wars to maintain his power over Europe. In 1806 he won a decisive victory over the Prussians at Jena. He defeated them again the following year in Poland. Napoleon forced them to give him control over their territories in eastern Europe.

The Russians had also fought against him in Poland, but he was more lenient with them because he wanted the czar to join him in an alliance against the British.

Napoleon decided to establish a blockade against British goods throughout Europe. By closing the ports of all the countries he'd conquered to British imports, he hoped to ruin the British economy. Napoleon also wanted the Russians to close their ports to British trading vessels. Because he didn't have direct control over their ports, he tried to convince the czar to join his blockade.

Although Russia was Britain's ally in the league, the czar made a secret pact with Napoleon. He agreed not to allow British trading vessels into Russian ports. The czar also would try to persuade Great Britain to make peace with Napoleon. If the British refused, he promised Napoleon he would declare war on Britain. Their pact became known as the Treaty of Tilsit.

Napoleon was jubilant. Two great powers, Austria and Prussia, had fallen to him, and Russia had pledged to betray her ally. Napoleon felt sure he would finally prevail over Great Britain. To completely block the British from trading in Europe, he invaded Spain and Portugal. This gave him momentary control over every European port from southern Spain to the Baltic Sea. Throughout his empire, Napoleon organized a blockade against British goods. Called the Continental System, it prevented the British from trading anywhere in Europe for several years.

Napoleon's blockade was ultimately unsuccessful. The British economy did not suffer as much as he had hoped. In 1812 he learned that Czar Alexander was permitting English imports into his country despite their pact. The czar was retaliating because Napoleon had installed his own brother-in-law as the crown prince of Sweden, even though by the Treaty of Tilsit Napoleon had agreed to support Russia's bid to rule that country.

Incensed by the czar's action, Napoleon made plans to invade Russia. Gathering the largest army ever assembled, he marched it across Europe. His Grand Army numbered over half a million men, conscripted from all parts of his empire.

Once in Russia, Napoleon was surprised to find village after village deserted. Vast stretches of the country had been abandoned by the Russians. With a growing sense of disquiet, Napoleon ordered his men to march on to Moscow. Near the city the Russians met him in battle at Borodino, but the Russians were defeated after a hard battle. Afterwards they offered no further resistance as the Grand Army approached Moscow.

When Napoleon's men saw the spires of the city in the distance, they rushed forward, crying "Moscow! Moscow!" They were happy to reach the Russian city after marching thousands of miles across Europe.

As they got closer, Napoleon hurried forward to the head of his troops. Scanning the legendary onion domes of Moscow, he shouted with joy, "There at last is this famous city! And about time!"

Napoleon marched into Moscow on September 14. He soon found that the long-awaited city was a ghost town, ransacked and deserted. That night a spectacular fire engulfed Moscow. It had

been set by the Russians under orders from the city's governor. Napoleon's soldiers shouted in alarm as they saw the flames, but they couldn't stop the fire because the Russians had smashed all the city's water pumps before fleeing.

For five days Moscow was ablaze. Two thirds of the city was destroyed before Napoleon's troops were finally able to occupy it.

Napoleon was uneasy. The czar had let him conquer Russia without waging another battle after the Russian defeat at Borodino. Czar Alexander had even abandoned Moscow without a fight. Anxiously, Napoleon sent him the terms he demanded for peace. Weeks went by without any response. Napoleon's soldiers were growing restless. Because the fire had burned down most of the houses in the city, the men had no shelter to protect them from the increasingly cold weather. Many were forced to go foraging for food, because Napoleon's provisions were running out.

His policy of rapid marches across wide expanses of land meant his troops had to travel lightly. As few supplies as possible were taken along on his campaigns. Napoleon's soldiers were expected to forage for food by pillaging the farms and towns they encountered on their marches. Because the Muscovites had fled with all their possessions, the soldiers had no food. In desperation, they began killing and eating their own horses.

Napoleon still hadn't heard from the czar a month after arriving in Moscow. The situation was growing critical. He knew his men wouldn't survive the Russian winter if they stayed in Moscow any longer without food or shelter. He ordered his advance scouts to locate the position where the czar was quartering his army, because he was sure he could defeat the Russians if he met them in a direct battle.

One of his scouts reported back several days later. "Sire," he said, "we believe the czar has withdrawn his troops much farther inland."

"What does that mean?" stormed Napoleon. "Didn't you find the enemy's camp?"

Trembling, the soldier answered, "No, Sire. Everything is deserted for miles."

"Are all the villages abandoned?" he asked the scout brutally. The strain of waiting for news from the czar had worn Napoleon down. Though he tried to appear as decisive and self-confident as usual, he was nervous.

"Yes, Sire. And the people set fire to their homes and to their crops before fleeing."

When he heard this, Napoleon suddenly understood the czar's strategy. He realized he had fallen into a trap. His Grand Army was stranded in the heart of Russia without any possibility of getting fresh supplies from France. His troops had to rely on what they could find in Russia, but the czar's orders to scorch the fields and desert the towns destroyed any hope of replenishing their supplies. Napoleon saw that the czar had let his troops march so far into Russia because the czar counted on the hard Russian winter to starve the Grand Army to death.

Napoleon realized he was defeated. He ordered a retreat on October 19, a month after his army's arrival in Moscow. The soldiers were happy to begin the march home to their families. But their joy was soon cut short when it began to snow. Because Napoleon hadn't planned on a winter campaign, the men didn't have any warm clothing. Exhausted and hungry, they trudged through deep snow. Daily, the snow piled into higher and higher snowbanks.

"Keep on marching," they urged each other. "Don't fall asleep. Just keep on going."

The men knew that if they gave in to the temptation to lie down and sleep on the snow, they would risk freezing to death. At first the soldiers shared overcoats and what little food they could find or rob along the way. Eventually, however, so many men starved or froze during the tragic march home, they were just left to die, unaided. Hundreds of thousands of men perished, marching across Russia.

The Hundred Days

Napoleon's campaign in Russia was the greatest disaster in military history. Napoleon's Grand Army of over half a million men was decimated. Some died at Borodino, but most were lost to the cold, to disease, and to malnutrition.

Because his army was shattered, Napoleon's enemies quickly banded together in a new alliance to take advantage of France's military weakness. The six members of the league — Spain, Portugal, Russia, Sweden, Austria, Great Britain and Prussia — threatened invasion on all sides. In addition the British Duke of Wellington was scoring a number of victories against the French forces stationed in Spain. He was driving them farther and farther north toward the French border. If he continued, Napoleon knew, he would invade France in a matter of months.

Napoleon didn't wait for his enemies to invade. Typically he went on the offensive, conscripting 350,000 new soldiers from within his empire. Although the French were mourning their war dead from his disastrous Russian campaign, he was still able to inspire them with a desire for victory against the allied armies.

"Soldiers!" he declared. "The immortal glory of our nation rests in your courage and your devotion. Let not our enemies defeat us and crush us under the yoke of injustice!"

His new recruits had no military experience. Many were barely sixteen years old. Yet they enthusiastically joined the army because the threat of foreign invasion had raised patriotism to a feverish pitch in France.

Napoleon marched his troops into Germany in the spring of 1813 to meet the enemy head on. His inexperienced army managed to defeat the allies in three successive battles. Even though the enemy had a far superior army, Napoleon's military genius and the bravery of his young soldiers made them victorious. However, despite a valiant effort, his forces were finally overwhelmed by the allies in a battle that lasted three days, at Leipzig in Germany. Called the Battle of Nations, it ended with Napoleon's defeat on October 18, 1813.

When he ordered a retreat from Leipzig, the allied armies pursued his troops back to France. Napoleon was able to fight off an invasion for several months, but on March 31, 1814, Paris was finally occupied by the allies.

Hoping for a miracle, Napoleon fled to Fontainebleau, a palace outside of Paris. He steadily refused to give up his throne, despite pressure from the allied armies for his abdication.

On the night of April 12, he tried to commit suicide by taking poison. Although he was violently ill, he recovered by morning. Later he wearily asked his aides to bring him the documents drafted by the allies for his abdication.

"Fate has decided I must live and wait for all that providence has in store for me. I'm condemned to live. Even death has betrayed me. It will take courage to endure life after all I've been through," he told them with resignation. Then, taking pen in hand, he added with a defiant shrug of his shoulders, "I abdicate, but I yield nothing."

He left Fontainebleau two weeks after he signed the Act of Abdication. In the courtyard of the palace, his faithful Old Guard — his elite corps of army veterans — gathered to say goodbye to him.

"Soldiers of my Old Guard," he told them, "for twenty years I've seen you always on the path of honor and glory. During the last few weeks you've been models of bravery and fidelity, just as in the years of good fortune. Farewell, my friends. Keep me in your memory. I will be happy when I know that you are happy."

"Long live the emperor!" they shouted, many crying openly, as he left.

Considering the hatred the allies felt toward Napoleon, the terms of their peace treaty were surprisingly generous to him. He was banished to the small island of Elba, near Corsica. Given the

title of prince of Elba, he had the command of a few ships and an army of eight hundred men. Napoleon also had an annual salary and the use of several homes on the island.

However, Napoleon grew irritated under the restrictions of his life at Elba. He thought he cut a ridiculous figure as the governor of the tiny island when, less than four years before, he had ruled an empire stretching from southern Spain to eastern Poland. Shortly after his arrival at Elba, news began reaching him that the French were dissatisfied with the ruler selected by the allied armies. He was the brother of Louis XVI, the king beheaded during the Revolution. The allies had wanted to restore the monarchy in France, but the candidate they chose soon grew unpopular in France. Louis XVIII was already disliked because he was a member of the despised Bourbon family. This fueled great resentment against him when he tried to eliminate the civil rights won by the Revolution.

Napoleon decided to exploit the political unrest in France. Daily he plotted his return to Paris. While seeming to occupy his time with the administration of Elba, he was actually contacting supporters in France who were eager for him to assume power again. The allied armies had whittled his empire back to the borders of France. His supporters believed only Napoleon could reconquer these territories and make France an empire again.

While Letizia Bonaparte was visiting her son at Elba, Napoleon confided to her that he was going to escape several days later by ship. At first she was upset by his plans to reassume power. Then, she looked him in the eyes and gave him a knowing smile.

"Heaven won't allow you to die by poison or in your bed, which would be unworthy of you, but with sword in hand," she said sadly. "Go, my son, and fulfill your destiny."

On the night of February 26, 1815, he fled Elba with a small army. Landing in France the next week, he marched north to Paris in twenty days. His army met cheering crowds throughout France. By the time he reached the capital, his troops had swelled to several thousand soldiers. Entire garrisons abandoned King Louis XVIII to join Napoleon's troops. In Paris, Napoleon reassumed the title of emperor.

Final Exile

On June 22, 1815, Napoleon was again forced to abdicate. Aware that the allies would be much harsher in their terms this time, he tried to escape to the United States. Napoleon hoped to get to America by booking passage on a merchant ship out of the French port of Rochefort, on the Atlantic.

In secret he fled to Rochefort, but when he arrived in the town, he learned that the British were blocking the port and wouldn't let any ship sail without first inspecting it to make sure he wasn't aboard.

Napoleon knew that if he surrendered to the allied armies, he risked execution or exile. However, if he attempted to flee by crossing France, he was certain of immediate execution, because the allies had ordered that he be shot on sight should he try to escape the country by land.

Napoleon decided to give himself up to the British authorities. On July 14, 1815, he boarded the H.M.S. *Bellerophon* in the harbor of Rochefort. On the deck he met Captain Maitland, the commander of the British man-of-war.

"I come to place myself under the protection of your prince and laws," Napoleon said.

Captain Maitland accepted his surrender. Under orders from the British government, he immediately set sail for Plymouth in England. For five hours Napoleon stood alone on the deck of the man-of-war as it sailed away from France. Glumly he watched the coastline of his beloved country recede in the distance. All of his hopes of recovering his empire were shattered, he knew, and he sensed he would never again see France. Respecting his desire for privacy, the British naval officers kept their distance while he searched the darkening skyline for the last traces of his country. Because they treated him well during the voyage, Napoleon hoped he might be exiled to England.

When he landed at Plymouth, however, Napoleon learned he was being sent to St. Helena, a remote island lost in the South Atlantic. The British chose it because he would have no possibility of escaping from it. St. Helena was a thousand miles away from the coast of Africa and six hundred from the nearest island.

Horrified, Napoleon protested, "I appeal to history! Don't send me to St. Helena!" But the British wouldn't be moved. On August 10 he left England aboard the H.M.S. *Northumberland* headed for St. Helena. Just over two months later, on October 17, 1815, he landed on the desolate island made of volcanic rock.

A few friends and a handful of servants accompanied him in exile. At first they tried to make the best of their life on the lonely island. As the years passed, though, they fought increasingly among themselves. Only Napoleon stood aloof from their quarrels. He remained solitary, just as he had been as a boy. When they tried to embroil him in their conflicts, he told them to leave him alone.

Brooding over his defeat at Waterloo, Napoleon decided to write his memoirs to justify his military campaigns, which had cost the lives of so many people. Though he was proudest of his conquests, he recognized that his greatest contribution to France had been the Code Napoleon.

After nearly six years of lonely exile, Napoleon died on May 5, 1821, of stomach cancer at the age of 51. In his will he had written: "I would like my ashes to rest on the banks of the Seine, in the midst of the people I so greatly loved." Despite his wishes, he was buried on St. Helena. Twenty years later, however, the British allowed his remains to be brought back to Paris, in state.

NAPOLEON'S SCHOLARS IN EGYPT

When Napoleon left to conquer Egypt in 1798, he took with him hundreds of artists and scientists to study the culture of the country. One percent of his military expedition was made up of scholars, including one composer and an astronomer. It was the first time a military campaign was undertaken with such a great number of scholars.

Napoleon was genuinely interested in scientific exploration, but he had also shrewdly realized its propaganda value the year before, when he had conquered Italy. As part of its war tribute, Napoleon had sent hundreds of masterpieces, including art works from the Vatican's holdings, back to the museums of Paris. This made the people of the city dramatically aware of his conquest in Italy. Napoleon knew that treasures from Egypt, considered exotic by Europeans, would have even more appeal in France.

After Lord Nelson destroyed Napoleon's fleet at Abukir Bay on August 1, 1798, Napoleon's army was stranded in Egypt for a year, because they were unable to get back to France by sea. Though Napoleon tried an overland route through the Near East, his forces were soon daunted by the vast deserts they had to cross. He ordered them to retreat to Egypt, which he had conquered.

While he administered the country, Napoleon's team of scholars gathered information on Egyptian culture. They studied every aspect of the country's life — from the fish in the Nile to the sand in the desert. They also measured the pyramids and other ancient monuments, such as the Sphinx. However, their greatest discovery happened by accident.

Near the garrison town of Rosetta, a French soldier found a stone that bore inscriptions in three languages — demotic, Greek, and hieroglyphics. Because ancient Egyptians used picturelike characters, called hieroglyphs, early scholars believed the characters stood for the objects they looked like. The Rosetta stone's significance became clear in 1821, when the French scholar Jean-François Champollion, knowing that the inscriptions were actually the same text in three different scripts, realized that hieroglyphs were alphabetic characters. Champollion's discovery made it possible to decipher hieroglyphics and unlock the mystery of the ancient Egyptian language.

The work that Napoleon's scholars did in Egypt benefited the Egyptians as well. Making a tour of the country, they drew the first complete map of Egypt. They were also the first to introduce printing to the Egyptians. The Egyptians' first published book was an excerpted version of the Koran, which had never been printed in Egypt before. Also, as Napoleon had predicted, the Egyptian artworks his scholars shipped back to France proved very popular at home, even inspiring an Egyptian style in interior decoration. The scholars' greatest contribution, however, was a nine-volume report, which they wrote on their return to France. It laid the base for the science of Egyptology, the study of ancient Egyptian culture.

A French medal commemorating the Battle of the Pyramids.

French scientists, members of Napoleon's campaign in Egypt, take measurements of the Sphinx. (Engraving)

THE CODE NAPOLEON

In 1800, when Napoleon was First Consul, he engaged a commission of the four most respected jurists in France to combine all the French civil laws into one code to simplify the judicial system. He closely supervised the drafting of this code, insisting that it be presented in a lucid and readable form. Called initially the Civil Code, it was decreed the law of France on March 5, 1803, and went into effect throughout the country the following year.

The code inspired the European nations in Napoleon's empire — such as Belgium, Italy, and Spain — to unify their own civil laws into one code. The Civil Code, later known as the Code Napoleon, eventually influenced legislation in countries that were not under his direct control. Its simple and precise structure was adopted in nations as diverse as Japan and Egypt. On the American continents, too, it influenced law in the province of Quebec, the state of Louisiana, and much of South America.

Although the Code Napoleon embodied some of the ideas of the French Revolution, it was essentially a conservative document, which preserved many of the laws in existence during the monarchy. It strengthened paternal authority in the family, recognized inheritance and property rights, and annulled the liberal divorce laws established during the Revolution. Nevertheless· it laid the foundation for the legal rights of French citizens, and it did guarantee a number of individual rights fought for during the Revolution.

Napoleon's Civil Code was his greatest contribution to France. Despite some changes it is still in use there today. Because of its worldwide influence, the Code Napoleon also instituted in other countries laws based on ideas of individual liberty conceived during the French Revolution. This legacy is considered one of the most important developments of the French revolutionary era.

Portrait of Napoleon as First Consul, painted by Jean-Auguste-Dominique Ingres in 1804. (Musée des Beaux Arts, Liège)

THE LOUISIANA PURCHASE

On May 2, 1803, Napoleon signed a treaty selling 827,987 square miles of land that France owned in North America to the United States. The United States paid nearly fifteen million dollars for this land, which stretched from the Gulf of Mexico north to Canada and from the Mississippi River west to the Rocky Mountains. This acquisition practically doubled the size of the United States. Fifteen states were eventually created from this territory.

Napoleon was well aware of the land's value. He had dreamed of forming a French empire in North America. However, his weak navy made it impossible for him to protect his territories so far from the European continent. The previous year, in 1802, he had tried to quell a rebellion in France's West Indian colony of St. Dominque, which is now the Dominican Republic, on the island of Hispaniola. Rebellious slaves had taken control of the island. When Napoleon's army came to stop the uprising, they were savagely attacked by the insurgents. Many of his soldiers also succumbed to fever in St. Dominque.

Napoleon realized the difficulty he would have in governing a North American empire. An imminent war with Great Britain convinced him he needed immediate funds for his war treasury. Also, when the United States made it clear that it would join the British in a war against France if he did not agree to sell the land, Napoleon decided to give up his North American territory. He understood the potential power of the new country and wanted the United States to remain neutral if he engaged in a war with Great Britain. When he signed the treaty, Napoleon observed with relish: "This accession of territory [by the Americans] affirms forever the power of the United States. I have just given Britain a maritime rival that sooner or later will lay low her pride."

Congress ratified the purchase of this territory on October 25, 1803. Two months later the United States took possession of it, which allowed American pioneers to settle in the new land. This acquisition became known as the Louisiana Purchase. It was one of the most important acts of Thomas Jefferson's presidency, because it permitted the westward expansion of the United States throughout the nineteenth century and greatly increased the resources available to the young country.

A view of the port of New Orleans, shown in an engraving of the period.

JOSEPHINE, THE CREOLE EMPRESS

On March 9, 1796, Napoleon married Josephine de Beauharnais. She was the penniless widow of an aristocrat guillotined during the Reign of Terror. Josephine nearly risked execution herself when she pleaded for mercy for her husband. Arrested and put in prison, it was only the sudden overthrow of Robespierre's government that stopped her from being sent to the guillotine.

Josephine grew up in Martinique, a French colony in the West Indies. She was a Creole, a native of the island but of French descent. When Josephine was a girl, one of her black slaves from Haiti predicted she would become a queen someday. Josephine liked to tell this story to her court when she became the empress of France.

She was very popular with her subjects because she had dignity and warmth. Her charm made them forgive her extravagances for Josephine was a spendthrift and always deeply in debt.

The imperial couple inspired a new fashion named the Empire style, modeled on ancient Rome and intended to recall its grandeur. Josephine was a great asset to Napoleon. He lost a great deal of popular support when he divorced her because she was not able to bear him children. Napoleon wanted an heir to continue his dynasty. He still loved Josephine, but his ambition proved stronger than his attachment to her. In 1810 Napoleon married the Archduchess Marie-Louise of Austria, the daughter of the Austrian emperor. The following year, their son, the king of Rome, was born on March 20, 1811.

Despite their divorce, Napoleon continued to visit Josephine at her estate outside Paris. When he was sent to Elba, she wrote asking if she could join him in exile, but she died on May 29, 1814, before she could leave France.

Portrait of Empress Josephine, painted by Pierre-Paul Prud'hon. (Louvre, Paris)

CHRONOLOGY

Napoleon Bonaparte's Life	Historical and Cultural Events
1769 August 15 — Napoleon Bonaparte is born in Ajaccio, Corsica.	**1769** May 1 — Arthur Wellesley, the future Duke of Wellington, is born in Dublin.
1789 Napoleon is made a second lieutenant in the artillery unit of a regiment garrisoned at Auxonne in France.	**1789** July 14 — Mobs storm the Bastille in Paris. Its fall marks the beginning of the French Revolution, which leads to the end of the monarchy in France.
1793 December 19 — Napoleon recaptures the port city of Toulon from the British. Three days later he is awarded the rank of brigadier general.	**1793** January 21 — King Louis XVI is executed. His Austrian wife, Queen Marie Antoinette, is beheaded on October 16.
1794 August 8 — Denounced by his fellow military officers for being a Jacobin, Napoleon is arrested and put in prison. Two weeks later the government declares him innocent of all charges and sets him free.	**1794** July 28 — Maximilien Robespierre, a radical Jacobin leader, is sent to the guillotine. With his death ended the Reign of Terror, during which thousands of people, accused of being Royalists, were guillotined.
1795 October 5 — By using cannons, Napoleon crushes a Royalist insurrection in Paris. In gratitude the Directory later appoints him commander-in-chief of the Army of the Interior.	**1795** A moderate government, called the Directory, is established in France. One of the five directors, Paul-François Barras, who had appointed Napoleon to defend Paris from the Royalists, becomes director in chief, after his victory over the insurgents.
1796 March 9 — Napoleon marries Josephine de Beauharnais. March 11 — He goes to war to drive the Austrians out of Italy.	**1796** John Adams is elected the second president of the United States. Thomas Jefferson is elected vice-president.

A print showing the storming of the Bastille.

Marie Antoinette, Queen of France, in a portrait by L.L. Perin Salbreux.

Horatio Nelson accepting the surrender of the Spanish after their defeat following the capture of Cape St. Vincent by the British.

Portrait of John Adams, the second president of the United States.

Napoleon Bonaparte's Life	Historical and Cultural Events
1798 May 19 — Napoleon sets out to conquer Egypt. Joining the military expedition are hundreds of scholars and scientists whom he hired to study Egyptian culture. July 21 — His troops defeat the Mamelukes at the Battle of the Pyramids.	**1798** August 1 — While Napoleon is fighting inland in Egypt, Lord Nelson destroys his fleet at Abukir Bay at the mouth of the Nile. This tactic leaves Napoleon's army stranded in Egypt for a year.
1799 November 9–10 — Returning to France, Napoleon overthrows the Directory. He has himself named First Consul of France.	**1799** The Rosetta stone, found near the garrison town of Rosetta by one of Napoleon's soldiers in Egypt, has inscriptions in three languages, including hieroglyphics.
1800 May 15–20 — Planning a surprise attack on the Austrians, who have again marched into Italy, Napoleon leads his army over the Alps in a rapid march. June 14 — Unprepared to fight, the Austrians are defeated at the battle of Marengo.	**1800** Thomas Jefferson becomes the third president of the United States, after defeating John Adams in the election. The federal offices are moved from Philadelphia to Washington, D.C., the new capital of the United States.
1803 March 5 — The Civil Code, drawn up under Napoleon's supervision, is decreed as the law of France. Later known as the Code Napoleon, it unifies all the country's civil laws into one systematic body of legislation.	**1803** May 22 — The Louisiana Purchase is ratified. By acquiring from Napoleon a tract of land extending from the Gulf of Mexico to the northwest, Thomas Jefferson doubles the size of the United States.
1804 December 2 — Napoleon crowns himself emperor in the presence of Pope Pius VII. The magnificent coronation ceremony is held at the Cathedral of Notre Dame in Paris.	**1804** Beethoven composes his Symphony No. 3, known as the *Eroica*, in honor of Napoleon. When he learns Napoleon has taken the title of emperor, he angrily dedicates his work instead "To the memory of a great man."

A public meeting at the time of the Directory in an engraving by Chavaignier.

A street in Philadelphia in 1790 (Historical Society of Pennsylvania).

Thomas Jefferson, the third president of the United States.

Ludwig Van Beethoven in a painting by Ferdinand Schimon.

Napoleon Bonaparte's Life	Historical and Cultural Events
1805 December 2 — Fighting against the Austrians and the Russians, Napoleon scores the greatest military victory of his career at the battle of Austerlitz.	**1805** October 21 — Napoleon's navy, under the command of Admiral Villeneuve, is destroyed by Lord Nelson at Trafalgar, off the southwestern coast of Spain.
1806–1809 The other great powers of Europe, threatened by Napoleon's conquests, join in a league against him. To destroy their alliance, he defeats the Prussians, the Russians, and then the Austrians in various battles. Only the British escape attack, since his weak navy prevents him from conquering Britain by sea.	**1806–1808** Conquering Spain and Portugal guarantees Napoleon's control over all European ports from Algeciras to the Baltic Sea. Hoping to destroy the British economy, he institutes the Continental System to block British vessels from exporting goods into any port within his empire.
1810 March 11 — Napoleon, after divorcing Josephine the previous year, marries the Archduchess Marie-Louise of Austria.	**1810** The Spanish painter Goya begins a series of etchings called *Disasters of War* about Napoleon's occupation of his homeland.
1811 March 20 — Napoleon's son is born. Napoleon gives him the title of king of Rome.	**1811** The Duke of Wellington drives Napoleon's forces out of Portugal.
1812 June 23 — Napoleon's Grand Army invades Russia. September 14 — His forces occupy Moscow, abandoned by Czar Alexander I. October 19 — Napoleon orders the Grand Army to retreat. The disastrous march kills thousands of his men, decimating his army.	**1812** Continuing his campaign against Napoleon's army in southern Europe, the Duke of Wellington defeats the French in a number of battles in Spain. In gratitude for having liberated Madrid, Goya paints the *Portrait of the Duke of Wellington*.
1813 October 16-18 — The allied armies defeat Napoleon at the battle of Leipzig.	**1813** October 7 — After marching triumphantly across Spain, the Duke of Wellington invades France.

60

A print showing Admiral Nelson dying from a bullet wound during the Battle of Trafalgar.

The Continental System: goods coming from Great Britain are burned by the French.

With Reason or Without from the series of etchings *The Disasters of War* by Francisco Goya. Paris, Bibliotheque Nationale.

The Duke of Wellington in battle.

Napoleon Bonaparte's Life	Historical and Cultural Events
1814 April 6 — Forced to abdicate by his allied enemies, Napoleon is banished to the island of Elba.	**1814** March 31 — The allied armies occupy Paris. They reinstitute the monarchy and establish Louis XVIII, the brother of Louis XVI, as the king of France.
1815 February 26 — Napoleon escapes from Elba. Returning to Paris, he reassumes the title of emperor after Louis XVIII flees Paris. June 18 — The Duke of Wellington defeats him at Waterloo in Belgium. August 10 — Napoleon is exiled to St. Helena, a remote island in the South Atlantic.	**1815** At the Congress of Vienna to determine the spoils from his defeat, the allies hear that Napoleon has escaped from Elba. They immediately form a new alliance against him. Declaring him an outlaw, they prepare a new military campaign to defeat him once and for all.
1821 May 5 — Napoleon dies on St. Helena, after nearly six years in exile.	**1821** Using the Rosetta stone, Champollion deciphers Egyptian hieroglyphics.

Louis XVIII, King of France (seated figure), at the balcony of the Tuileries. Painted by L. Ducis.

The Rosetta stone, which made it possible to decipher hieroglyphics.

BOOKS FOR FURTHER READING

Napoleon by Anthony Masters, McGraw-Hill Book Co., New York, 1981.

Napoleon and the Battle of Waterloo by Frances Winwar, Random House, Inc., New York, 1953.

For Advanced Readers:

Napoleon, Man of Destiny by Herbert J. Gimpel, Franklin Watts, Inc., New York, 1968.

Napoleon by Manuel Komroff, Julian Messner, New York, 1954.

INDEX